EDGE
BOOKS

✦ INTO THE GREAT OUTDOORS ✦

BEAR HUNTING
For Kids

BY MATT CHANDLER

Consultant:
Este Fisher
Member and Legislative Representative
Virginia Bear Hunters Association

CAPSTONE PRESS
a capstone imprint

Edge Books are published by Capstone Press,
1710 Roe Crest Drive, North Mankato, Minnesota 56003
www.capstonepub.com

Library of Congress Cataloging-in-Publication Data
Chandler, Matt.
  Bear hunting for kids / by Matt Chandler.
      p. cm. – (Edge books. Into the great outdoors)
  Includes bibliographical references and index.
  ISBN 978-1-4296-9901-3 (library binding)
  ISBN 978-1-62065-693-8 (paperback)
  ISBN 978-1-4765-1522-6 (ebook PDF)
  1. Bear hunting–Juvenile literature. I. Title.
  SK295.C37 20132
  799.2'7784–dc23   2012019493

Editorial Credits
Brenda Haugen, editor; Gene Bentdahl, designer; Eric Gohl, media researcher;
    Kathy McColley, production specialist

Photo Credits
Alamy: canadabrian, 12; AP Images: Ric Feld, 19; Capstone Studio: Karon
Dubke, 8, 11, 25; Getty Images: Colin Archer, 22; Newscom: akg-images,
6, MCT/Sam Cook, 16, PacificCoastNews/Dan Callister, 21; Shutterstock:
2009fotofriends, 3, airn, 18, Dave Allen Photography, cover, David Dohnal,
7, Erik Mandre, 4–5, gnohz, 29, Scenic Shutterbug, 26, Wyatt Rivard, 1;
SuperStock: Science Faction, 14

Printed in the United States of America in Brainerd, Minnesota.
092012   006938BANGS13

TABLE OF CONTENTS

CHAPTER 1

THE BIG, FURRY HULK

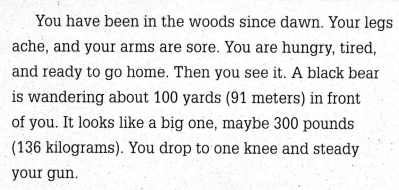

You have been in the woods since dawn. Your legs ache, and your arms are sore. You are hungry, tired, and ready to go home. Then you see it. A black bear is wandering about 100 yards (91 meters) in front of you. It looks like a big one, maybe 300 pounds (136 kilograms). You drop to one knee and steady your gun.

You struggle to remember everything you were taught. You know the bear could trot away at any second. The clock is ticking. You can feel your heart racing with excitement.

After one final adjustment, you squeeze the trigger. The shot is perfect. The bear staggers and stumbles forward, heading for cover in the woods. But it won't get far. You follow the bear's tracks in the snow to claim your prize.

FACT
Black bears are not always black. They can also be shades of red, brown, tan, and white. But the two most common colors are brown and black.

History

People have hunted bears since prehistoric times. Bears provided early people with much more than food. Hides were used for clothing and blankets. Bear bones could be made into tools.

In North America, American Indians used bear fat as cooking oil. The fat was also turned into oil for lamps and used as medicine.

Popular Bears to Hunt

The most common bear to hunt in North America is the black bear. But don't be fooled. Just because the black bear is commonly hunted doesn't mean it is easy to bag. Black bears are shy animals. They can hide in densely wooded areas that are hard for hunters to reach.

An average adult black bear is about 35 inches (89 centimeters) tall at its shoulder. It weighs between 200 and 400 pounds (90 and 180 kg). But some black bears grow bigger. Black bears weighing more than 600 pounds (270 kg) have been found. Although black bears are big, they are fast. Taking down a black bear is a big challenge.

Another bear commonly found in North America is the brown bear. Brown bears include the Alaskan brown bear and grizzly bear. Both are **protected species** and cannot be hunted in most states.

brown bear

FACT
The largest black bear ever taken down was recorded in 1885. The animal weighed 802.5 pounds (364 kg).

protected—guarded to be kept safe from harm; laws usually protect animals classified as protected species

species—a group of animals or plants that share common characteristics

CHAPTER 2

PREPARING FOR THE HUNT

Bears are very difficult animals to hunt. You could hunt every weekend during bear hunting season and never see one. When you do see a bear, you need to have the right equipment to take it down. Having a gun or bow you can handle is important. **Blinds** and camouflage clothing will also help you succeed.

Choosing a Gun and Ammunition

The right gun can mean the difference between getting a bear and watching it escape. You need a gun powerful enough to take down a bear with one shot. If you shoot a bear with a low-**caliber** weapon, such as a .22, it could escape. The animal's thick fur and muscle will protect it and minimize the damage. Choose at least a .30-caliber rifle.

Your choice of ammunition is also important. You need a bullet that will tear through a bear's thick hide. You want the bullet to leave a hole big enough that the bear continues to bleed. If the bullet hole is small, the animal's fur can soak up the blood. The fur can become matted down and slow or stop the bleeding. This can give the bear time to escape.

blind—a hidden place from which hunters can shoot

caliber—the size of a weapon's bullets

There are many different kinds of ammunition. The type you choose depends on your gun. But you want a bullet that can travel at least 2,000 feet (610 m) per second. For example, a .222 Remington cartridge travels 3,140 feet (957 m) per second. A .30-30 Winchester will also do the job, traveling 2,200 feet (671 m) per second. If you try taking down a 400-pound (181-kg) bear with a bullet that is traveling too slowly, you may go home empty-handed.

Bowhunting

Hunting bears with a bow and arrow is not common for young hunters. It takes a perfect shot with a bow and arrow to take down a bear.

If you want to take on the challenge of bowhunting for a bear, you need to pay attention to a bow's draw weight. A draw weight of 35 pounds (16 kg) means it takes the same strength to draw the bow back as it would to lift 35 pounds (16 kg). Most states require that hunters use bows with minimum draw weights of 35 pounds (16 kg) to hunt big game. This law protects the animals. A slow arrow can injure a bear but not kill it. If you are a beginner, practice with a 25-pound (11-kg) bow on a range. Build up your strength and accuracy until you can handle a 35-pound (16-kg) bow.

Wear blaze orange over your rain gear to help other hunters see you.

Other Gear

Because many bears spend a lot of time on rugged land, wearing good hiking boots is important. You may hike miles into the woods to find a good hunting spot. It is also important to dress for the weather. Carry rain gear and layer your clothing in case the weather changes.

A bear can pick up a scent 5 miles (8 kilometers) away. If a bear smells you, it will quickly hide. You can buy special hunting clothing that absorbs your scent and keeps it from reaching a bear's nose.

You may also want to use a scope. A scope connects to your gun or bow and acts like a magnifying glass. It helps you see bears from a long distance.

Other important tools to have in your bag are a map of the area, a compass, and binoculars. Each will help you track a bear. And a map and compass will keep you from getting lost. You should also carry a small first-aid kit in case you get hurt. Carry plenty of water with you to avoid getting dehydrated.

BUYING A SCOPE

The type of scope that you will use depends on your weapon and your personal choice. But there are a few basic things your scope should have.

✦ **Anti-fogging glass.** Early spring mornings are a great time to hunt bears. But cool morning air in the woods can create fog and mist. Moisture can get into your scope and fog up the lens, making it impossible to see. Anti-fogging glass cures that problem.

✦ **A large objective lens.** The objective lens is the glass at the front of the scope. The bigger the objective lens is, the greater the amount of light that can get in. The best time to find bears is at the beginning or end of the day when it isn't very light out. Having a lens that allows in more light can help you spot a bear.

✦ **A strong build.** If you buy a cheap scope, you may regret it. The woods are a rugged place, and your scope should be sturdy. Your scope is going to take a lot of abuse, and you want it to work when you need it.

HUNTING TECHNIQUES

bear tracks

You have your gear along. You have the perfect hunting spot. You and the others in your hunting group arrive before dawn. Now the real work begins. Bears are really good at avoiding humans. Their powerful sense of smell alerts them to your scent from far away. So what are the best techniques for taking down the big one? It starts with preparation.

14

Tracking

You can tell a lot from bear tracks. A track's size can help you figure out how big the animal is. A 5-inch (13-cm) track from a front paw tells you the bear is at least 150 pounds (68 kg). Smaller prints or many sets of prints likely come from a female bear or her cubs. But even though they can tell you a lot, bear tracks are tough to spot. The best time to find a bear by following tracks is in the winter after a fresh snowfall.

You can beat a bear's powerful nose by tracking into the wind. If the wind is blowing in your face as you hike, it is taking your scent away from the bear. This technique will give you a chance to sneak up on a bear undetected.

Since bears are **elusive** animals, some hunters use blinds to gain an advantage. A blind is a structure that hides you from the bear and lets you surprise the animal. A blind is a good tool if you are in an area where you know a bear lives or is visiting often. The disadvantage of using a blind is that it limits your hunting area. That's why many hunters prefer to track bears. Because bears are often on the move, a hunter who keeps moving may have better luck.

elusive—clever at hiding or being able to escape

Dung

It may sound gross, but you can learn a lot from looking at a bear's dung. A large pile is most likely from an adult bear. Soft dung means it is fresh, and the bear may be nearby. You can also inspect the dung to see what is in it. Pieces of fruit or undigested peels may tell you where the bear is eating. If you find dung with a lot of fruit in it, look for a nearby fruit orchard. It might be a good place to set up and scout.

Tree Markings

A bear stands on its back legs and scratches trees to mark its **territory**. Tree scratches offer two clues. First, they tell you a bear has been there. They also tell you about how big the bear is. If you measure how high the claw marks are, you can estimate a bear's height. A bear may also rub its body against a tree, which can leave fur behind.

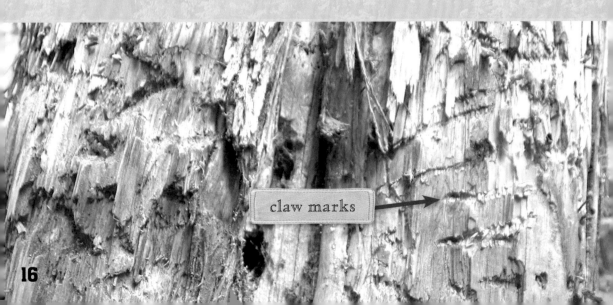

claw marks

USING A BAIT BARREL

Bears eat a lot. Because they sleep for much of the winter, bears search for food to fatten up before winter. They also wake up in the spring extra hungry. These behaviors can give you a big advantage if you hunt with a **bait barrel**. But before hunting with a bait barrel, check your state's laws. Some states don't allow hunters to bait bears. And some hunters don't think baiting bears is sportsmanlike.

To make a bait station, start with a 55-gallon (208-liter) barrel. Chain the barrel to a tree so the bear can't steal it. Then you are ready to mix bait. There are many ideas about what makes the best bear bait. Usually it is a combination of sweet and rotten foods. Add lots of sweets, such as old doughnuts and brown sugar to the barrel. Toss in some rotten meat or fish. Add more sweeteners such as honey or molasses, and mix everything up. Clear the space around the barrel, and pour cooking grease around it. The grease has a smell that will draw in bears. A bait barrel should be refilled every day. Adding new food to it will create new smells to attract bears.

territory—an area of land that an animal claims as its own to live in

bait barrel—a large barrel filled with food to attract hungry bears

Shot Placement

If you do track down a bear, the hardest part
remains. It can be difficult to get a clean shot. If
the bear is in deep woods, trees may block your
shot. Hunters often pass on trying to shoot a bear
because they can't get a shot they believe will kill it.

The best way to take down a bear is with a
shot just behind the shoulder. A well-placed shot
should find the bear's heart, killing it quickly. If you
are bowhunting, aim for the bear's ribs. Even the
sharpest broadhead arrow won't go through a bear's
shoulder blade.

TAKING YOUR BEST SHOT

There is a big difference between practice shooting at a **range** and taking down a bear in the wild. One of the biggest challenges is accounting for the wind. Even though a bullet shot from a rifle travels quickly, the wind can change the path your bullet takes. Hunters have to make adjustments in their aim to account for the wind.

range—a place for shooting at targets

FACT
So how do you make sure you don't miss your shot when the time comes? Plenty of range shooting practice helps. It also helps to improve your vision with the use of a scope.

range shooting

After the Kill

Once you are sure the bear has been hit, your work isn't done. You have to track the bear into the woods. Most bears won't fall from a single shot. They will try to escape before dying somewhere else. You must follow the blood trail and find your bear so you can field dress it quickly. Field dressing involves removing the animal's organs and cooling the meat as fast as possible. If you don't field dress the bear right after it dies, the meat can spoil.

Before you begin to track the bear, load your gun. The bear may still be alive and a second shot may be needed to kill it. Always make sure the gun's safety is on before you begin tracking to avoid any accidents.

You also need to be alert. A wounded bear can be more likely to attack as you are tracking it. If the bear survived, the first shot may not have been well-placed.

FACT
If you are attacked by a bear, experts say you should punch the animal in the nose. A bear's nose is very sensitive.

blood trail

Once you locate the bear and make sure it is dead, you must start to field dress it. First, remove the bear's organs. Removing the organs helps a carcass cool faster and keeps the meat from spoiling. The best way to cool the meat is to hang it from a tree. That will allow the air to surround the meat and cool it more quickly. In warm weather you need to field dress especially quickly. After as little as one hour, the meat can begin to spoil. If you are hunting in the winter you will have more time.

CHAPTER 4

HUNTING SAFETY

You are holding a weapon capable of taking down a huge bear. If you don't respect the dangers of hunting, you could get seriously hurt. But if you follow basic hunting safety guidelines, you can enjoy hunting with little risk.

Know Your Target

The best hunting places are often thick with trees and brush. When you see movement in the distance, be sure you know what you're aiming at before you shoot. Many states require hunters to wear blaze orange to avoid being mistaken for a big game animal. Even if it isn't a law where you live, wearing blaze orange is a good idea.

Weapon Safety

A gun or bow can be a dangerous weapon. As you are walking, keep your gun pointed toward the ground. You will be tracking bears through deep woods and could trip and fall. Keep your gun's safety on until you are ready to shoot at a bear. A weapon that goes off accidentally could injure you or another hunter.

If you are bowhunting, never walk with an arrow loaded in your bow. It might be tempting to load your bow because you want to be ready to shoot as soon as you have a bear in your sights. But a quick shot isn't worth the risk of tripping and landing on a razor-sharp arrowhead.

Stay Alert

Although bears do attack people, it is rare. Bears most often attack if they are startled. Female bears are more likely than male bears to attack people to protect their cubs. Keep your distance if you see a bear with cubs.

Some hunters carry bear spray to injure an attacking bear. If you come across an aggressive bear, don't run away. Slowly back away from the animal. Many experts believe that if you run, a bear is more likely to attack because it sees you as **prey**.

prey—an animal hunted by another animal for food

FACT
About 750,000 black bears live in North America, but there is only an average of one deadly attack each year. You are 120 times more likely to die from a bee sting than from a black bear attack.

CHAPTER 5 CONSERVATION

FACT
Former President Teddy Roosevelt loved to hunt. He was also a conservationist and is credited with starting several conservationist programs.

An important part of being a hunter is being a good **conservationist**. Hunters should respect the land they are hunting on. If you carry in food and supplies for a hunt, clean up. Bottles, cans, and other garbage can harm the environment. Metal bullet casings can get into nearby streams and harm fish. They can even get eaten by animals, making them sick.

Some hunters cut down trees and clear brush in their favorite hunting spots. But clearing land hurts the environment and should never be done. If you cut down trees, you take away homes for the birds. You also take a food source from animals that eat berries and leaves from the bushes and trees.

Another way to be a good conservationist is to join hunters' groups. These groups often raise money that is used to protect the **habitats** of bears and other animals. The World Wildlife Fund is one of the biggest conservationist organizations in the world. It protects **endangered** animals such as the grizzly bear.

You can be a good conservationist by following the rules of hunting. Each state sets its own rules. There are restrictions on when you can hunt and what bears you can kill. These laws protect the bear population from being overhunted.

conservationist—someone who works to protect Earth's natural resources

habitat—the natural place and conditions in which an animal or plant lives

endangered—at risk of dying out

A Worthwhile Challenge

Many hunters believe a bear is one of the hardest animals to hunt. With its great sense of smell, a bear can avoid hunters. A bear's strength makes it a threat. Its size makes killing the animal with a single shot a challenge. But hunters say all of these things are part of the thrill.

Many hunters spend years tracking bears without ever killing one. Hunting is a sport that requires more than just being a good shot. You must study the land and know every habit of the bears you are hunting. You must be a skilled tracker and know how to field dress your kill.

You won't become an expert hunter overnight. But the work you do will be worth it when you have a bear in your sights and make the perfect shot.

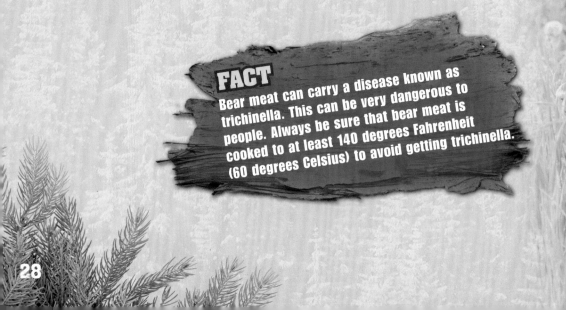

FACT
Bear meat can carry a disease known as trichinella. This can be very dangerous to people. Always be sure that bear meat is cooked to at least 140 degrees Fahrenheit (60 degrees Celsius) to avoid getting trichinella.

GLOSSARY

bait barrel (BAYT BAYR-uhl)—a large barrel filled with food to attract bears

blind (BLYND)—a hidden place from which hunters can shoot

caliber (KA-luh-buhr)—the size of a weapon's bullets

conservationist (kuhn-sur-VAY-shun-ist)—someone who works to protect Earth's natural resources

elusive (ih-LOO-siv)—clever at hiding or being able to escape

endangered (in-DAYN-juhrd)—at risk of dying out

habitat (HAB-uh-tat)—the natural place and conditions in which an animal or plant lives

prey (PRAY)—an animal hunted by another animal for food

protected (proh-TEK-ted)—guarded to be kept safe from harm; laws usually protect animals classified as protected species

range (RAYNJ)—a place for shooting at targets

species (SPEE-sheez)—a group of animals or plants that share common characteristics

territory (TER-uh-tor-ee)—an area of land that an animal claims as its own to live in

READ MORE

Howard, Melanie A. *Bowhunting for Kids*. Into the Great Outdoors. North Mankato, Minn.: Capstone Press, 2012.

Klein, Adam G. *Hunting*. Outdoor Adventure! Edina, Minn.: ABDO Pub., Co., 2008.

MacRae, Sloan. *Big-Game Hunting: Bears, Elk, and Other Large Animals*. Open Season. New York: PowerKids Press, 2011.

INTERNET SITES

FactHound offers a safe, fun way to find Internet sites related to this book. All of the sites on FactHound have been researched by our staff.

Here's all you do:

Visit *www.facthound.com*

Type in this code: 9781429699013

 Check out projects, games and lots more at
www.capstonekids.com

INDEX